Stepping Out

Kat Bourne

ISBN # 978-0-9848178-8-7

For further information please contact:

Theovette Publications
P.O. Box 221161
Hollywood, FL 33022
www.theovette.com
email: contactus@theovette.com

Stepping Out

Poetry and Prose
Kat Bourne

Dedicated to my son JJ, my family and friends.

Her Light

There's a radiance that travels with her wherever she goes.
When she walks into a room it seems to take on a special glow.
Even when she's outside and walking under the sun's rays
Her glimmer and sparkle are evident even during the day.

While the moon and stars glisten in the nighttime sky
They seem dim compared to her and her burst of light.
Like a shadow the light trails along wherever she may be.
The brightness outshines the dark and surrounds her body.

She seems unaware of the aura that sparks when she passes by.
Her smile at those who notice makes her light even more bright.
She quietly thinks to herself I'm doing fine and okay.
I'm happy, I love myself and my inner peace is here to stay.

She Fell in Love Today

She fell in love with someone today.
It's a person she's known her whole life.
That person is beautiful and amazing;
Has a special spirit and is creative, smart and kind.

She's always genuinely liked this person
But didn't always appreciate their gifts and beauty.
Now she's convinced that this person is a treasure;
More valuable than precious stones or other quality things.

Sometimes when she's out in the world
She can't wait to be alone with her best friend.
To tell them how truly amazing they are
And that she's got their back to the end.

She and her love have had some rough days
And loving this person has taken some time.
Now this person has her heart fully and unconditionally.
The person is imperfect but 100% ok in her mind.

Her mirror reflects the person that she loves.
She is the person she fell in love with today.
She accepts and trusts herself completely.
It's a love and friendship that will never go away.

Dance Girl

Don't be a wallflower.
Get up and dance.
It doesn't matter if you have two left feet.
Go on - give it a chance.

You don't need a partner.
Just get up and start moving girl!
Don't worry about who might be watching.
Get on out there and give it a whirl.

Just move your body with the beat.
If you want to go ahead and sing along.
Who cares if you're out of tune?
Dance, sing, enjoy life – it's your only one.

Stepping Out

I'm stepping out – taking detours from the journey that is my life.
Checking and rechecking out the world already available to me.
I don't need to travel to some far off place.
Plenty of amazing things are surely within my reach.

The beach is only a few miles away.
I'll walk on the sand or let the water soothe my body.
Sniff in the scent of the salted water and air.
Enjoy the feel of the cool fresh breeze.

I'll go to the park and admire beautiful trees.
Many of them are filled with nice green leaves.
Bring a book, my music player and headphones too.
Sit in the grass in shade, listen to music or enjoy a good read.

I've seen flowers along the way before,
But I've rarely stopped to enjoy the colorful show.
I'll enjoy the reds, yellows, pinks, whites, violets and more.
Smell jasmine, roses, gardenias, others – give pleasure to my nose.

I'll visit museums and view beautiful and interesting works of art.
Borrow books, music, movies or catch events at the library.
See a play performed on stage or a movie at the theater.
Listen and dance to live music - at many locations it's free.

I'll raise my eyes to the beautiful blue sky and give thanks
Embrace the warmth, brightness and wonderfulness of the sun.
In the evening I'll dance under the magnificent stars and moon;
That should be so much fun.

I'll take in a sunset or sunrise or seek out rainbows after the rain.
See animals at the zoo or observe birds and butterflies fly.
Learn something new or taste a food or drink I've never had.
Other things to discover; they are out there for me to find.

Dance to the Music

She's seeking peace - wants a good night's sleep;
Fighting against demons that won't leave keeping her awake.
She's trying to focus on happy memories and thoughts -
Instead of those that cause tears to flow down her face.

She's forgiving herself for bad choices that she's made
And for enduring toxic conditions from day to day to day.
Dumping baggage that keeps her tired and worn down.
Leaving heaviness and darkness for a lighter, happier place.

She's battling the desire to just lie down and die
And praying for the willpower to fight to live.
Staying strong when things go wrong.
Remembering she's special with very much to give.

She's determined to shed the mask she wears to the world
Reclaim her once glowing soul so it matches her outer smile.
Unleash the dismal inner spirit that has taken control
And shine from within for a while.

Once upon a time she would dance the night away.
Music was a dear old comforting friend.
That's where she decides to start:
Return to the music. Yes, that's where she'll begin.

Nourish your dreams

Nourish your dreams.
Pay attention to them each and every day.
Encourage them as if they are people you care about.
Neglected and forgotten dreams might decide to slip away.

Don't be afraid to add more dreams to the ones that exist.
You're entitled to have as many dreams as you like.
Dreams likely don't mind sharing space with other dreams.
Shower them with conviction and hope so that they don't die.

Believe in your dreams with all your heart and soul.
Fight for them with every ounce of your power and will.
Embrace and stimulate your dreams while you still have breath.
When you're gone your dreams become nil.

Live it!

Walk like you've won the lottery.
Carry yourself like you have no cares and worries.
Take off your shoes and run barefoot on the beach's sand.
Go for a swim or let grains of sand run through your hands.

Let raindrops fall down on your face.
Travel to an unfamiliar place.
Dance and sing to your favorite songs.
Press replay again and again and each time sing along.

Turn off the TV and get lost in a book until the end
Call or go visit a family member or friend.
Feel the warmth of the sun outside or fly a kite
Play a sport or game with others, skate or ride a bike.

In cold weather drink hot chocolate, coffee, soup or tea
Enjoy the snow or stay inside and find some company.
Smile and say hello to a person you don't know.
Relish your life's moments as if they are a special show.

Pursue and capture your hopes and dreams.
Believe in yourself - you can be whatever you want to be.
Make the best out of what you've got from day to day.
Remember to always keep the faith.

Destiny

I'm feeling it – I think it's time
For me to spread my wings and take flight.
I'm zooming out and taking control of my life.
Who knows - I might just reach the sky.

Many dues I have paid
Along my life's journey to where I am today.
I will get over obstacles that block my way.
I'm moving forward and stepping out on faith.

I will withstand any kind of weather;
Be it rain, sleet, snow, summertime heat, whatever.
I'll do what's needed 'til all the pieces come together.
Success will be mine even if it takes forever.

There have been detours and missteps by me.
Still I've learned most things are as they should be.
I sense my goals are within my reach.
I believe any day now I'll arrive at my destiny.

Brown Eyes

My palm against my son's palm
Skin touching skin hand to hand
His fingers now outstretch mine
No longer a little boy
Not quite a man

Brown eyes brown eyes
Looking at him I see
The love of my life
With brown eyes like honey

I'm standing next to him
His shoulders now even with mine
I think of when I held him
In my arms
For the very first time

Brown eyes brown eyes
Looking in them I see
My finest work of art
With brown eyes like honey

And one day not so far away
He'll be looking down on me
When I'm old and gray
He's not a boy but a man
With brown eyes like honey

Brown eyes brown eyes
Looking into them I see
The love he has for his mom
Those brown eyes like honey

Throwback

I was walking alone through this big grassy field
On a beautiful, cloudless, warm sunny day
When I noticed a little girl dressed in a pink frilly dress
Who was following me as I went on my way.

Before I knew it she caught up and grabbed my hand
And happily skipped along with me with a smile on her face.
I had a sense that I had seen her somewhere before
And being with her felt like a natural state.

Even when the girl and I walked through prickly weeds
She was able to find beautiful colorful flowers.
She was cheerful and free and an unlikely comfort to me
As we hung out and passed through the hours.

We left the field and began walking through town
And I seemed to be going back to familiar places.
Everyone was quiet except me and my new friend
Even though I thought I saw familiar faces.

My buddy and I hopscotched and jump roped.
We really enjoyed ourselves as we laughed and played.
I was a bit uncomfortable because I was a stranger
But then she said my mother's, my father's and even my name.

We splashed in the rain that suddenly came down that day
And danced without inhibitions to music in the streets.
I felt a little taken aback when she said
That she loved me, was proud of me and was happy to see me.

Somehow we ended back in the field where we first met.
We hugged each other, said goodbye and I asked her name.
She suddenly disappeared into the night
After saying that our names were the same.

On Track

It's definitely time for me step up my game
And get myself charged up and into gear.
For way too long I've lived in a neutral state
But now I'm letting go of all my doubts and fears.

I'm gonna tap into all of the qualities
That have been naturally given to me.
I'm smart, I'm talented, I'm attractive, I'm great.
As the saying goes I'm ready to be all that I can be.

Oh, yeah I'm ready yeah I'm ready
And on my way to hitting the big time
And when I get there like I know I will
I'm gonna get everything that's meant to be mine.

I'm gonna slide some shadow on my eyes
And smooth some red or pink gloss on my lips.
My cheeks will be highlighted with blush
And a slinky pretty dress will cling to my hips.

I'm gonna invoke my sassy, sexy feminine side
And get outa that dreary plain jane mood.
I will be slipping on my dancing shoes
And getting my butt into the groove.

Oh, yeah I'm ready yeah I'm ready
And on my way to hitting the big time
And when I get there like I know I will
I'm gonna get everything that's meant to be mine.

No more will I be down with the blues
'Cause life's way too short for that.
I've got a whole lot to offer the world
And believe it baby I know I'm on the right track!

Butterfly

You're looking at your reflection in a mirror
Which like an image in a circus' funhouse glass
Is distorted and unreal.
You despise what you see.
But it is your own mind
That creates something warped and fuzzy.

Unfairly you begin to dissect yourself
Down to each and every piece.
You criticize your eyes, your mouth,
Your body, nose, legs, even your knees.

If your eyes were taking in what was real
The reflection that they'd view
Is something extraordinary, fantastic, amazing, original, gorgeous.
Your eyes would see the truth.

You are like a caterpillar
That exits an egg and gently crawls along
Leaves and twigs feeling its way around
And exploring its new world.
For you there will come a day when you wake up
And realize you're an exquisite, beautiful girl.

In this stage of your life
It is commanded that you
Compliment each and every feature
Each and every day;
Because all of them put together
Make up your wonderful body and face.

A moment will occur when
You will go into yourself like a cocoon and
Inside your soul a process will take place.
You will begin to grow -
Begin to love yourself and soon
A stronger you you will come to know.

And like a butterfly that emerges
From its shell in colorful glory
Flapping it wings proudly and
So freely in the wind
You will learn to appreciate
The glorious body and skin you're in.

On that particular day
When you look in the mirror
And stare back at the girl in the glass
You're going to love what you see.
You will wrap your arms around yourself
And shout out loud it's great to be me!

Butterfly.

More to Me

There's so much more to me
Than what the outside world sees.
I've had more than my share of sadness and pain
And I have experienced many very dark days.

There have been mornings when
I didn't want to leave my bed.
The thought of facing the world
And my problems filled me with dread.

Lonely moments even
When folks were right there
And I still felt as if I really didn't belong –
Didn't fit in anywhere.

There have been occasions in my life
When my painted lips were curled in a smile
And other people assumed I was happy
When all the while
My heart has ached;
Feeling as if at any moment
It might just shatter and break.

Sometimes it's felt as if glass
Has penetrated and pricked the lining of my soul.
I acted the part of self-assurance and contentment
And within I shivered like
Someone standing out in the cold.

I've laughed out loud on days
When I've wanted to cry.
Pretended to be someone
On top of the world
While my inner spirit was down in the dumps
And seemed to slowly die.

Yet I've risen up every morning because through it all
I have hope and faith,
And although I've had difficult times there have been lots of
fulfilling and wonderful days.

I've been lifted and supported by people – angels - who have had my
back in life.
Yes, I've had some trying times but I'm not ready to give up my
fight.

Dark Cloud

Dark cloud, dark cloud, just let me be.
Dark cloud, dark cloud, stop hovering over me.
Dark cloud, dark cloud, please let the sun come on out.
If there's a storm headed my way just let the rain start falling
down.

Dark cloud, dark cloud, you've stayed around for way too long.
Go ahead and do what you want to do so I can move on.
If you think I will let you take my joy and confidence away,
Think again 'cause I know you'll eventually be gone some day.

So dark cloud until you decide that you'll be going somewhere else,
I'll stop focusing on you and concentrate on myself.
Even though I won't forget that you're still somewhere nearby,
My eyes can look in a different direction where there's some light.

Dark cloud, dark cloud, I see that you are about to change.
You're opening up and when you do I will dance in the rain.
For now I'll just accept you since you're a part of my life,
But as soon as you're gone I plan to bask in the sunshine.

My Return

Bored, it might be time to join the human race again.
Make some new or reacquaint with old friends.
This isolation gig has gotten old.
Now I'm thinking of getting back in the fold.

I check the time and realize only a few minutes have gone by.
I gotta get a move on if I'm to have a different life.
Work, TV, the web, listening to music alone are not quite doing it for me.
They are lacking in the intimacy that I'm beginning to seek.

Sometimes I think I wouldn't mind having a dude wrap me up in a loving embrace.
Kiss me on the lips while gently stroking my face.
But then the coziness of my soft blanket and a good book in my hand
Comforts me and engages me so I'm not sure if I want a man.

Some people say that we're not meant to be just one;
That we're happier when we're with others and being loved.
I'm starting to think there might be some truth to that.
There could be some who'd be glad to see me if I come back.

Crossroads

I'm at a crossroads in my life.
Don't know if I should go left or right.
Do I go up or down?
Make my way north or south.

Never thought I'd be road blocked in this part of my life's page.
Figured things would've merged smoothly by the time I reached
this age.
Can't believe I'm questioning who I am, who's the real me
And wavering about like some girl in her teens.

I suppose I should stand up and take my share of the blame.
My life's position could be due to questionable choices I've made.
I'm not having any pity parties for myself.
I will step it up and make the best of the years I have left.

I'm going to straighten up my shoulders and hold my head up high.
I'll exude confidence and grace and my smile will be bright.
It won't be long until I have everything in place.
Varoom I'm revved up and already out the gate!

Music Man

Hey music man, go ahead and do your thing.
Please sing to me – I want to hear my favorite song.
It's awesome seeing you with your amazing voice and cool swag.
I can watch and listen to you all night long.

I'm here because the music just takes my cares away.
For a few hours I dance like no one else is here.
The music transports me to another zone.
I become a dancing fool with nothing to fear.

I feel alive when you and the band rock the beat.
You guys really know how to liven up a place.
When you slow it down to a romantic slow song
I become lost in the smooth sounds – I just meditate.

So music man thank you for a beautiful night
And for sharing some of your time.
I've been entertained and really enjoyed myself.
Music man you always blow my mind!

Believe in Me

Believe in me
Though you might not see
In to the future and
What I'm gonna be
Be be be be be be bop

Stay with me
Though I'm not in flow
One day before we know it
I'll be bringing in the dough
Pa pa pa pa pa pa pop

I can feel it comin'
And I want you around
So I can share it all with you
When my stuff gets off the ground
La da da da da de dum

I know it's bound to happen
I'm positive I'll make it far
I want my baby there
When I become a superstar
Fe fe fe fe fe fi fum

It might be tomorrow
Sometime next or in a few years
With you by my side
I ain't got nothin' to fear
Rah rah rah rah yo yo yo

You've always been there
Through the thick and thin
As long as we're together
I'm sure we're gonna win
1234 here we go

Strip

Baby, I'm gonna strip for you tonight.
I'm about to bare it all for you to see.
Right before your two eyes I'm getting naked.
Be prepared to observe the real, unmasked me.

It's gonna be a fascinating night, sweetie.
I'm letting it all hang out and sharing everything I've got with you.
All traces of makeup will be wiped clean from my face.
In the next few hours you will witness me showing you my truth.

Secrets will be revealed that I've never told anyone else.
There might be some crying and tears that fall.
You'll hear about my hopes, dreams and plans for the future
And be welcomed in places where with others I've put up walls.

My heart will be exposed as if it lives outside my chest.
My soul, my spirit, my story will not be spared.
I will ask bold questions of you – yes you play a role in this too.
I'm taking things to a level where before I have never dared.

I will revel in the joy I've found in this love that we have.
Express my gratitude to you for getting and loving me as I am.
Honey, I trust you with my life.
That's why I'm taking it all off tonight for you, my man

Your smile

Oh, how I love your smile!
It really makes my day.
Some mornings I start out feeling just blah.
One smile from you and I'm doing okay.

Your smile is like one of those wonders of the world.
A brilliant star that shines and illuminates from far away.
It radiates like the afternoon sun.
My soul and heart are touched when your smile comes my way.

Your smile is like a rare masterpiece.
A priceless gem that's too precious to be sold.
I'll take your smile over any high priced jewelry.
Yep, your smile is something special to behold!

Hometown

Their part of town ain't the one with picket fences painted white.
It ain't the one where even the dog has a nice crib outside.
There ain't no huge backyards with fluffy green grass,
Or private at home swimming pools where kids swim and splash.

There ain't no fancy expensive cars parked in paved driveways,
Or wide tree lined streets where the children go out to play.
There ain't no basketball or tennis courts right there on folks' land,
Or daddies going to work in nice suits with briefcases in their hand.

Where they're from some boys have not lived to become men.
Some girls have had kids while they were still children.
Tourists are told to avoid the area where they sleep at night
But this is where they call home and try to thrive and survive.

Some might think parents there don't have hopes and dreams
That their kids might someday have more than what they've seen.
But the parents there want their children to learn, grow and play;
Have sweet dreams when they snooze and many wonderful days.

Behind the doors in their hood there's joy not just misery.
There are people who go to work and school and cook and eat.
There's laughter, music, dancing and lots of love and care.
On the inside they're the same as anyone else from anywhere.

Stepping Out II

I'm stepping out - gotta get up get up get up!
After work time has become dead time – I'm in a rut rut rut.
I've been letting life pass by me - it's flashing right on by me.
Need to push myself on out the door and get free free free.

Feel the hot kiss on my face of the sun sun sun.
Head over to the beach where I'll have some fun fun fun.
Take off my shoes and run next to the waves on the sand.
Let the water embrace my body, feet and hands.

Stroll along my hometown streets enjoy the breeze breeze breeze.
Sit under the shade of trees with their pretty green leaves.
Smell the aroma of pretty flowers, grass and food being cooked
While exploring and checking out my neighborhood.

Gaze at the beautiful blue sky sky sky.
Watch the beautiful birds and butterflies fly fly fly.
Listen to birds sing sing sing.
Take pleasure in the simple things life brings.

Adore the moon's glow shining so bright.
Wake up again, start brand new with the glorious sunlight.
See the world with a new set of eyes eyes eyes.
Tell monotony and lifelessness goodbye bye bye.

Chef Thug

If he wanted it
He would get it

He was a hard core thug
Dealing drugs in the street
Pounding on folks
Like they were pieces of meat

He dropped out of school
By the time he was ten
He had no plans to live by the rules
He knew that even then

If he wanted it
He would get it

As a kid he stole from the stores
And shook down other little boys
He had no problem at all
Snatching other children's toys

By the time he was twelve
He had been in and out of juvie jail
Put his hard working mother
Through all kinds of hell

If he wanted it
He would get it

At eighteen he was a participant
In an armed robbery
He was arrested and sent to prison for 10 years
Discovered how life is when you're *really* not free

They assigned him a dishwasher job
During his third year behind bars
He began watching the cooks prepare food
And learned to make meals dudes lined up for

At the age of twenty eight
He was released and decided to go clean
He applied for a job at several restaurants
And became a high class chef in number sixteen

If he wanted it
He would get it

Homeless

Night before yesterday the cardboard box she calls home fell apart due to severe water damage following an overnight summer rain... everything she owned was ruined.

Yesterday she arrived late at the soup kitchen and missed her one nourishing, hot meal.

Yesterday a stray dog tried to bite her and also swiped and ran off with half a hamburger she found on a fast food table.

Yesterday a cop shooed her from a park bench she'd been napping on.

Last night she slept in an abandoned building.

This morning she found a new cardboard box to call home.

Today she arrived early at the soup kitchen and ate a nourishing, hot meal.

Today a lady bought an extra hamburger at a fast food restaurant and gave it to her.

Today a nice policeman picked her up and took her to a shelter.

Today she received clothing and shoes at the shelter.

Today she met with a counselor who offered to help her find a job and complete her college degree.

Tonight she had dinner at the shelter and is sleeping in a bed.

Tomorrow.

Hip Hop Mom

She's dicing onions for
the homemade spaghetti sauce
being served with pasta and salad for dinner
in her spacious, beautiful suburban home.
The classical music she loves
soothes her as the onions bring tears to her eyes.
Her head springs up as she hears but barely
the pulsating beat that she does not appreciate but believes is hip
hop.
She tenses as the sounds become louder
and loom closer to her home.
A car's sound approaches - the engine's purring commingles with the
blasting music and rapid harsh language now very near.
Apprehensively and quietly she walks to
her living room and
discreetly peeks through
the curtains.
Immediately she recognizes the red Mercedes sports car parked in
the driveway.
She stares wide-eyed at her teenage son, Jason Silverberg, who is
waving his hands and bouncing his head to the
rhythm of the sounds.

Twins

Bounce, bounce, bounce, swoosh!

"Senior, Lavarius Jones, has just scored a three pointer, making his high school state champs!" the sportscaster exclaimed. "Lavarius has received several great offers from colleges around the state and country. He has accepted a full academic and sports scholarship to join the Florida State Seminoles."

Later...

Pop, pop, pop!

"Lavarion Jones, twin brother of Lavarius Jones, MVP of the state high school basketball championships, has been shot during an apparent brawl between rival gangs," the news anchor announced. "Lavarion has been allegedly identified as a member of one of the gangs; he has been previously arrested several times. He is expected to survive but it will take months of rehabilitation for him to recover from his injuries. Sources say prior to leaving school during his sophomore year, Lavarion had been attending the performing arts high school where he excelled in vocals and classical piano. Police Captain Richard Jones, the twins' father, has indicated that he will issue a verbal statement shortly."

Identical twins.
Different roads.

All American Girl

Sally Stone with blond hair
Gorgeous baby blue eyes
Her daddy's princess
Cheerleader and tennis star
Valedictorian
Popular
Sheltered

Bored -
she met up with the wrong dude
at a dark club.
He introduced her
to a new, exciting, dangerous world
and took her to a place where
she became unrecognizable
even to herself.

Victoria and Jordan

In her inner city project bedroom Victoria Washington sprays on Channel No. 5 perfume. She tosses her freshly done auburn human hair weave and applies a third coat of fire-engine red lipstick to her full lips.

Victoria smiles at her reflection in the mirror and says, "You go, girl! 40 years old and ya still got it goin' on!"

Victoria exits her room, knocks twice and opens the bedroom door of Jordan Washington, 13, who's doing his homework: an essay on Shakespeare's *Romeo and Juliet,* geometry, and a science fair project that's due in several weeks.

Jordan's eyes move from his computer screen to the mirror attached to his desk. He sees his mother dressed in a shiny leopard print mini skirt, halter top and very high-heeled shoes. He waits for her to speak.

"Ladies night at the Twilight," sings Victoria. She steps toward her son and kisses him on the cheek.

"Hey handsome!" she says. "Probably won't be up when you leave for school in the mornin' so leave a note on the frig of what you want for dinner. Gon' get me some shut eye before I head off to my evenin' shift at the hospital tomorrow night. But right now I'm steppin' out to have a lil bit of fun off on my night off."

She peers through a telescope in Jordan's room which is pointed toward a window. "Can't really see too much from here with this telescope," she says. "I think it's time for us to go check out that awesome moon and stars again with this thing. It's been a while since we've gone over to the beach to look at the sky. The next time I have a night off and you don't have school the next day we'll do that. Get somethin' to eat, see a movie and then check out the moon and stars. Lata Gata! Love ya, Jordie!" She pats him on the head, kisses his cheek and hugs him.

"Yeah, that stuff sounds good," says Jordan. "Love you, too."

Jordan hears the front door click open and then close. "Moms," he sighs and resumes his homework.

The Preacher

And the preacher rose
from his throne at the
head of the church
and walked toward the microphone
which was placed conveniently
in the center of the stage...The
congregation was sitting
patiently with sweaty faces,
partially closed eyes and
crossed, uncrossed legs
waiting...The preacher
reached his destination point,
removed his handkerchief
and wiped his brow...Then
he grabbed the microphone
and spoke into it very
softly, almost a whisper,
and several of the people
were forced to lean forward
to hear what he had the say...The
preacher's voice
began to rise a little bit higher
and suddenly he was shouting...The organist
who had been shaken from a nap
wiggled his fingers and soon
there was music...The
people began a'clappin'
and
a'singin'
and
a'dancin'...Then the preacher

abruptly stopped speaking
and walked back to his chair...The
music slowly faded
out...The organist returned to
his previous state...The
people retrieved their fans,
hankies and cooled off their bodies
and wiped their faces...They
leaned back against the pews;
crossed, uncrossed their legs
and
the church just
stood.

Addiction

He wants to give up the addiction that's captured his body and soul.
It's got a firm grip on him and its holding on extremely tight.
Refusing to let go the addiction has become almost a part of him.
It's very seductive and deceptive and helping to ruin his life.

When he's at it it feels so good
But after the high comes this incredible low.
The brief pleasure he gets is not worth it.
Deep down this is something that he knows.

There are times he believes he can escape.
Just break away and leave this bad habit alone;
But the addiction is so powerful and strong.
He's weak when fighting against this hypnotizing foe.

The addiction has created problems with family and friends.
Caused him to lose things dear to his heart.
It has cost him money he really doesn't have.
This addiction is tearing his world apart.

He says to himself today will be the last time.
Tomorrow comes and he's able to hold off a bit.
Then that thing slips back into his mind.
He's back at it again – takes another hit.

Jack

Life's battles have beaten Jack down
With an artillery that's stronger than one man.
He's retreated to the ocean side
Where the calmly rolling waves
Beckon him like a lover's welcoming hands.

The black sky and bright stars surround him
As the darkened water flows.
First as large foam filled gusts in the distance;
Then as spurts that meet him at the shore.
Like a playful friend the waves tickle his bare feet and toes.

Life changes when you least expect it
And in the darkness and silence of the late night sky,
Sorrows, regrets, low times
Usually kept at bay and dead during the day
May creep up and decide to come back to life.

In the vast wide-open sky a wall of light appears:
It is similar to a large movie screen.
Images like a mirage emerge before Jack's eyes.
He sees that it's his life playing out before him
And is stunned as he watches and hears long ago scenes.

He sees his family, mother and father
As they surround him – there he is as a baby.
His mom and dad's smiles and doting eyes
Are like beacons of light
Exuding love, excitement and glee.

He sees himself as a happy young child
Who was able to learn many things with ease.
Adult Jack watches the proud faces
Of his parents when he starts learning how to read
At the age of three.

Life changes when you least expect it
And in the darkness and silence of the late night sky,
Sorrows, regrets, low times
Usually kept at bay and dead during the day
May creep up and decide to come back to life.

In the darkness he sways from side to side
Like the palm trees' leaves.
His face is gently brushed
And his arms and legs caressed
By the alluring and cooling breeze.

He observes the elementary student that he was:
His teachers' pet – he was like a star.
An artist, great student, good friend,
Well-mannered, witty and polite.
It was predicted that he would go very far.

Life changes when you least expect it
And in the darkness and silence of the late night sky,
Sorrows, regrets, low times
Usually kept at bay and dead during the day
May creep up and decide to come back to life.

The man Jack cringes as his life begins to change.
He sees it before his own eyes.
There he is as an adolescent and teen
Who begins to smoke, steal
And stay away from home at night.

He views his mother
Who is worried and in emotional pain,
And his father as he drives along unfamiliar streets.
Jack observes the frustration on his dad's face as he
Searches for him in vain.

Life changes when you least expect it
And in the darkness and silence of the late night sky,
Sorrows, regrets, low times
Usually kept at bay and dead during the day
May creep up and decide to come back to life.

The moon glows and the stars twinkle and shine.
The stars seem to be whispering inside his head.
He thinks they're laughing - taunting and encouraging him
To enter the water
And end the life he's lead.

Older Jack watches himself as a young adult
In drug and alcohol induced hazes.
He neglects and abuses the women
Who attempt to love him.
He's responsible for the torment on their faces.

Life changes when you least expect it
And in the darkness and silence of the late night sky,
Sorrows, regrets, low times
Usually kept at bay and dead during the day
May creep up and decide to come back to life.

Next he observes recent arguments with coworkers
On days following all night alcohol binges in bars.
He sees his traffic tickets spread out like playing cards
And the after effects of several accidents he's caused.
There's damage done to people as well as the other cars.

Tears begin to rush down his cheeks
And he begins to uncontrollably weep.
He drops to the sand.
Exhausted and emotionally spent
He shortly falls asleep.

Life changes when you least expect it
And in the darkness and silence of the late night sky,
Sorrows, regrets, low times
Usually kept at bay and dead during the day
May creep up and decide to come back to life.

He awakens to the brightness of day
And the black water is now blue-green.
A cloudless, azure sky surrounds him
And the sun has replaced the moon.
Jack begins to reflect on what he's seen.

Then a stranger approaches Jack.
He sits and joins Jack on the sand.
Jack is cautious and wary
When the stranger smiles at him
And speaks to him as if they were friends.

The stranger reveals details of his life.
Tells of triumphs and tragedies.
He lost his children in a car crash.
He was diagnosed with cancer and his name is Bill
Through the hard times he struggles to find some peace.

Life changes when you least expect it
And in the darkness and silence of the late night sky,
Sorrows, regrets, low times
Usually kept at bay and dead during the day
May creep up and decide to come back to life.

Bill unexpectedly embraces him.
He smiles and looks directly at Jack.
Tells him that he's found ways to fulfill his life.
He's volunteering at a children's hospital today.
Said he believes it helps to give something back.

Jack feels much better than he felt last night.
He gives Bill his phone number and name.
He says, *Call me sometime if you wanna hang out or talk.*
Thanks for listening, Jack, says Bill
And for sharing part of your day.

No problem, Jack replies. *And thank you.*
Man, you don't know what you've just done for me.
Really nice to meet you, Bill.
Same here, Bill responds. *Glad I came here for a morning walk.*
The men shake hands, hug and leave the beach.

Life changes when you least expect it
And in the darkness and silence of the late night sky,
Sorrows, regrets, low times
Usually kept at bay and dead during the day
May creep up and decide to come back to life.

Later Jack visits his parents
Whom he hadn't seen in years.
They unconditionally welcome him
And he is thrilled and comforted
By their joy and happy tears.

Even later in the day Jack decides
That there are changes he wants to make.
He contemplates giving up drinking
And to start considering the feelings of others.
He thinks the world is not such a horrible place.

Life

Life may not seem always easy and fair
It might not fulfill all your dreams
You might hustle, fight, do all you can
And still not get all you want and need

It might seem every road you take
Becomes a u-turn, dead end or is blocked
You can't seem to find the key to success
The good life you seek is always locked

Darkness and doubt invade your mind
And you can't seem to find any light
You ain't sure which way to go next
Believing nothing will ever go right

Long hard nights can turn into daylight
The weather won't always be gloomy and gray
Troubles that life brings you won't last forever
Chances for change come with every day

Some might not see the good things you possess
But there will be those who do
Just keep living and doing and trying
Things are bound to turn around for you

There will be battles that you fight
And you might not always have the winning place
Feel good that you have done your best
And got no plans to get out the race

Long hard nights can turn into daylight
The weather won't always be gloomy and gray
Troubles that life brings you won't last forever
Chances for change come with every day

Riding out the Storm

Life can be like a hurricane
With rain coming down so hard and fast
You try to hide or
Winds blowing so rough they knock you down
You can complain knowing there's
Nothing you can do to change it
Or just wait until the worst part is over and
Get back out there
And play in the sunshine under the rainbow